DISCOVERING ANCIENT TECHNOLOGY

DISCOVERING THE TECHNOLOGY OF ANCIENT ROME

LINDSEY LOW

Cavendish Square

Published in 2024 by Cavendish Square Publishing, LLC
2544 Clinton Street, Buffalo, NY 14224

Portions of this work were originally authored by Charlie Samuels and published as *Technology in Ancient Rome*. All new material this edition authored by Lindsey Lowe.

Website: cavendishsq.com

Children's Publisher: Anne O'Daly
Design Manager: Keith Davis
Designer: Lynne Lennon
Picture Manager: Sophie Mortimer

Picture Credits
Front Cover: iStock: piola666 br; Shutterstock: Berti123 t, Stephen Seibel br.
Alamy: Chris Hellier 29; istockphoto: 37; Public Domain: Arthur Barlow 38, Luis Garcia 34, 42, 43; Ad Meskens 5; Shutterstock: ansharphoto 6, Joe Borg 20, Pantera 39, Rieke Photos 22, Rebecca Rye Photography 29; Thinkstock: istockphoto 1, 7, 10, 15, 16, 40, 41; Photodisc 14; Photos.com 32, 33, 36.

Cataloging-in-Publication Data

Names: Lowe, Lindsey.
Title: Discovering the technology of ancient Rome / Lindsey Lowe.
Description: Buffalo, New York : Cavendish Square Publishing, 2024. |
Series: Discovering ancient technology | Includes glossary and index.
Identifiers: ISBN 9781502669421 (pbk.) | ISBN 9781502669438 (library bound) |
ISBN 9781502669445 (ebook)
Subjects: LCSH: Technology--Rome--History--Juvenile literature. | Rome--Civilization--
Juvenile literature.
Classification: LCC T16.L69 2024 | DDC 609.37--dc23

CPSIA compliance information: Batch #CSCSQ24: For further information contact Cavendish Square Publishing LLC at 1-877-980-4450.

Printed in the United States of America

CONTENTS

INTRODUCTION

The stone, brick, and concrete buildings of ancient Rome were a demonstration of the Roman Empire's power and wealth.

The ancient Romans were great builders. Some remains of their walls and bridges, aqueducts, straight paved roads, and elaborate villas can still be seen across the world. However, construction was only one aspect of technology that shaped the Roman empire. There were also advances in farming and food production, textiles, and the manufacture of spectacular glassware. Technology often develops in a series of small steps, rather than in great leaps, and the ancient Romans adopted many ideas from earlier peoples, such as the Greeks.

ROME: ITS RISE AND FALL

The citizens declared Rome to be a republic in 509 B.C.E., and so began its rise to power. Over 300 years Romans dominated the whole Italian peninsula and parts of modern Spain. Another 300 years of warfare brought virtually the whole Mediterranean under Roman rule. After Augustus declared himself emperor in 27 B.C.E., the Roman Empire extended across much of Europe until C.E. 476, when Rome's western territory in Europe fell to the Visigoths. This book introduces readers to important examples of the technology that lay behind this remarkable period of power.

Roman homes had hypocausts, spaces beneath the floors filled with hot air from a furnace, which heated the rooms above.

TECHNICAL KNOW-HOW

This arch in the Italian city of Volterra was built by the Etruscans, the original rulers of the town of Rome.

Before the ancient Romans, the Etruscans and ancient Greeks had dominated the eastern Mediterranean and colonized parts of southern Italy. The Romans did not need to invent technology from scratch. Although they were great inventors, they borrowed, copied, and improved upon knowledge they learned from other peoples.

The Etruscans built large cities with roads, sewers, and water systems. They used aqueducts to bring fresh water to their cities. They also developed metallurgy, the use of metals. Their public buildings used the arch and the vault. The Romans would use and improve all these techniques.

BORROWING FROM THE GREEKS

From the Greeks, the Romans took a love of culture, such as art, music, and poetry. But the Romans also used Greek ideas about architecture. Their shipping was based on Greek vessels. They used everyday Greek technology, such as minting coins and making glass. But some Greek science, particularly mathematics, was too sophisticated for the Romans.

Roman ships were based on the vessels ancient Greeks had used to trade in the eastern Mediterranean.

CONSTRUCTION

Roman builders understood the physical forces that supported walls and roofs. They used stone, timber, marble, and concrete to create domes, arches, and amphiteathers. Such buildings were a sign of the strength and power of the empire. Some structures still stand today.

BUILDING A BASILICA

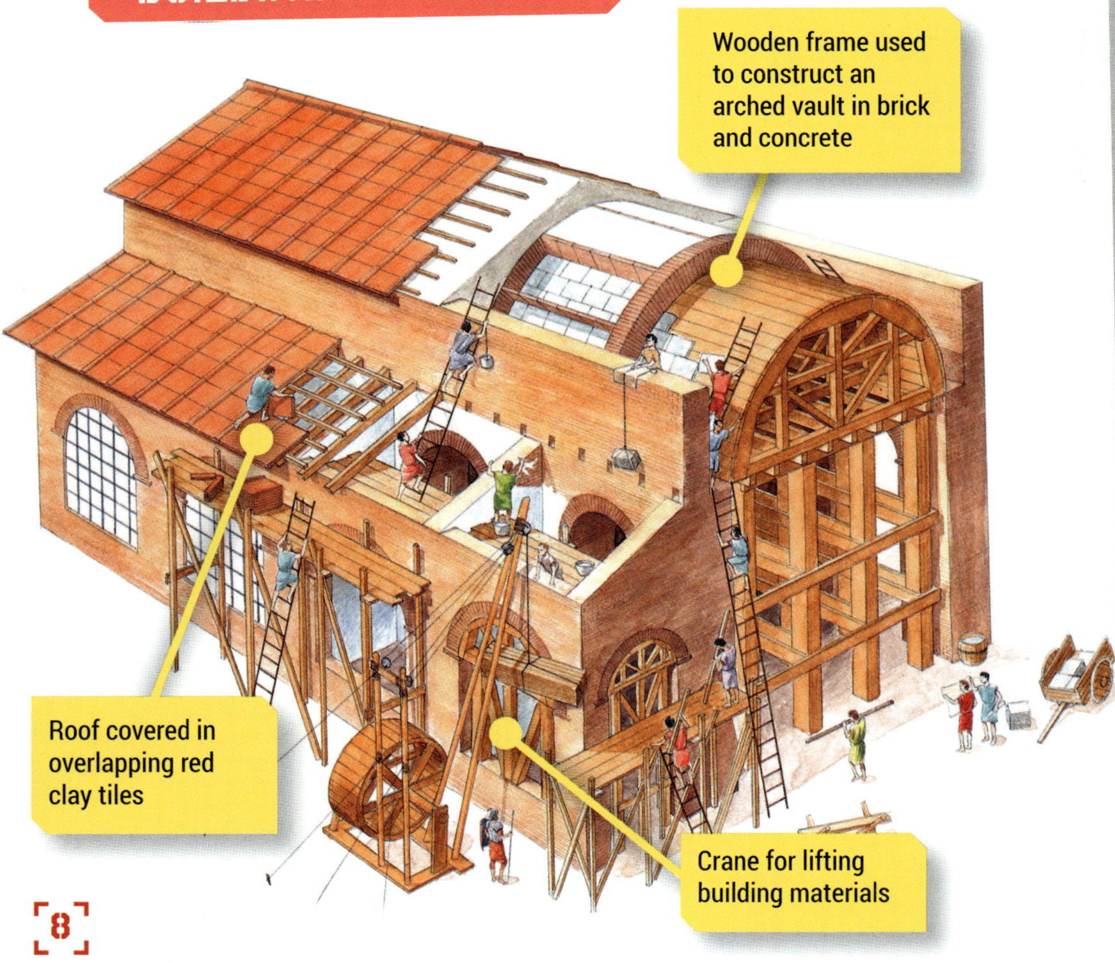

HOW TO...

The Greeks and the Etruscans had used arches in building. The Romans perfected the stone arch. An arch uses sideways forces to hold downward weight. Once its keystone is in place, it becomes remarkably strong. Roman builders used arches to build strong but light aqueducts, bridges, and arenas.

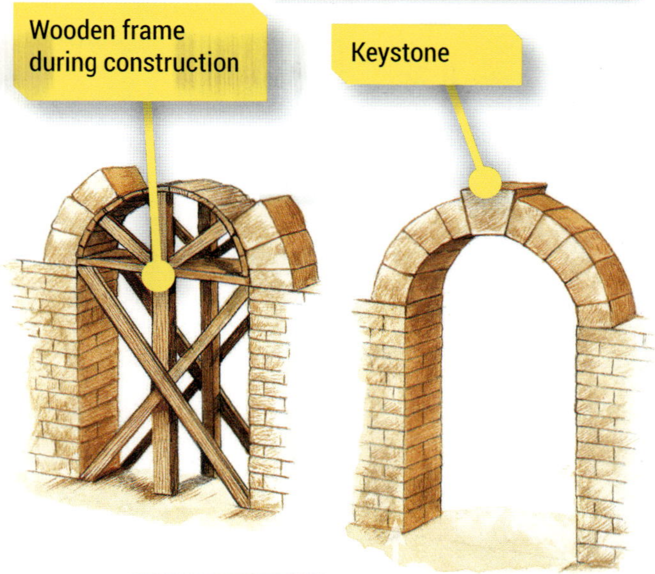

The Romans built the first cities across Europe. They constructed large public buildings for government and temples for worship. They built luxury villas for the wealthy and tall tenement blocks for the poor. They were expert water engineers and every city had public baths. Aqueducts brought clean water to towns and drains took sewage away.

THE CITY OF ROME

At the heart of the empire was Rome itself. It had the best examples of Roman architecture, such as the Colosseum and the Pantheon. Completing such building projects needed the labor of huge numbers of slaves from throughout the empire.

TECHNICAL SPECS

» The Romans developed the use of concrete for building; they mixed a volcanic ash called pozzolana with rubble to produce a light but strong material.

» Concrete made it possible for the ancient Romans to invent the dome. The massive dome of the Pantheon in Rome remains the largest of its type in the world.

» The firing of clay to make bricks was improved. Mobile high-temperature kilns allowed bricks to be introduced across the empire.

» The Romans used small squares of colored glass—mosaics—to create elaborate decorations for the floors of luxury villas and public buildings.

THE PANTHEON

The Pantheon in Rome is one of the city's most spectacular buildings. It was constructed for Emperor Hadrian between C.E. 118 and 125 and used advanced building techniques. It was probably originally built as a temple for Roman gods.

The recesses inside the dome helped to reduce its weight and also let the concrete dry more quickly.

The Pantheon is a rotunda, or drum shape, with a dome. The interior is based on a sphere: the rotunda is 142 feet (43 m) across and the top of the dome is the same height above the floor.

FEAT OF ENGINEERING

The dome is the largest example anywhere of an unreinforced concrete dome. It was designed to be as light as possible. It is 21 feet (6.4 m) thick at the bottom but 3 feet 9 inches (1.2 m) thick at the top. The builders used basalt to make the concrete at the base of the dome but pumice stone at the top, which is a much lighter material.

TECHNICAL SPECS

» To support the building's weight, its foundation walls are 24 feet (7.3 m) thick and sink 14 feet 9 inches (4.5 m) into the ground.

» The builders used heavy basalt to make the concrete at the base of the dome, but much lighter pumice stone in the concrete at the top.

» A ring of brick arches around the top of the rotunda walls helps to support the weight of the dome.

» The concrete of the dome is full of recesses to reduce its weight.

» The building materials and techniques used to lighten the weight of the dome reduced the stresses acting on it by as much as 80 percent.

LOOK INSIDE

ROMAN VILLAS

Wealthy Romans had comfortable country villas that were warm in the winter and cool in the summer. The houses were designed using the latest technology, with a central open atrium, or hallway, and rooms for cooking and sleeping. They also had communal bathrooms.

INSIDE A ROMAN VILLA

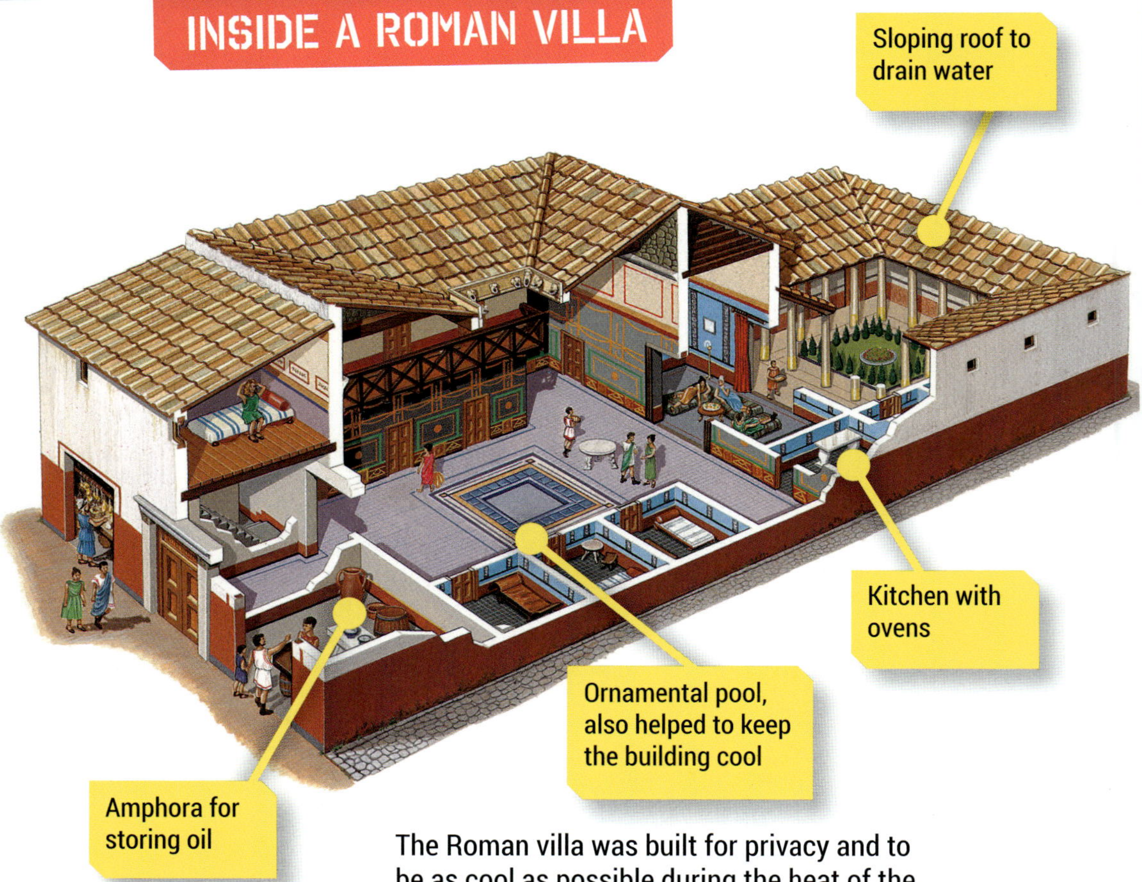

The Roman villa was built for privacy and to be as cool as possible during the heat of the Italian summer. Its walls were decorated with plaster and the floors often featured a mosaic.

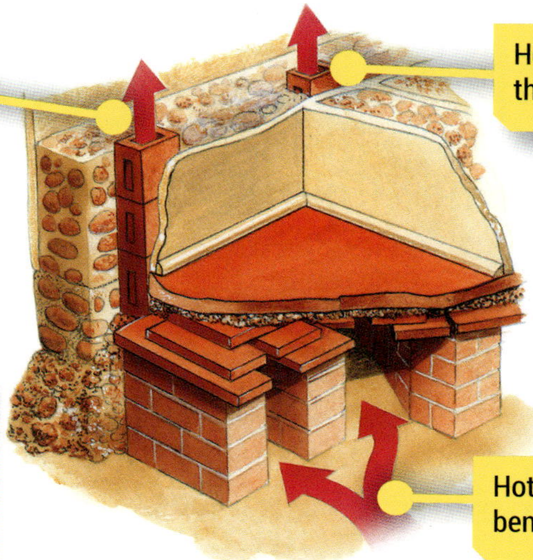

The hypocaust drew hot air up from a fire under the building's floors and up through its walls.

Roman villas had kitchens with brick-lined ovens, rooms for bathing, and even a bathroom. Roman ovens burned wood or charcoal. Slaves also kept a furnace burning. It heated water for bathing and also supplied heating to at least one room in the villa. Hot air from the furnace passed through underfloor passages, then escaped through flues in the walls. The system was called a hypocaust.

SHARED RESTROOMS

The restroom was not a private space, as it is now. It had a row of seats that were used by more than one person at a time. Running water flushed away the sewage.

TECHNICAL SPECS

- Villas were built from brick covered with plaster; the Romans perfected the mass production of clay bricks.
- Roofs used two types of red tiles: flat tegulae covered the surface; the vertical joins between tegulae were covered by semicircular imbrexes.
- Roman homes were designed to make the most of the natural light.
- The roofs slanted downward over the atrium; that allowed rainwater to collect in the central pool and kept the building cool.
- In the countryside, villas used rainwater or rivers for water; in the town, running water came into the home via pipes.

THE COLOSSEUM

The Roman Colosseum, originally named the Flavian Amphitheater for the family name of the emperors who built it, was a triumph of technology. It was built between C.E. 72 and 80. Seats for 50,000 spectators were arranged in tiers around a central space called the arena. Popular events included gladiatorial contests.

The arena no longer has its floor, so the ruins of the basement, or hypogeum, are clearly visible.

The walls of the Colosseum used a circular series of arches to support the weight of the spectators inside.

ENTERTAINMENT ARENA

The Colosseum staged shows from gladiatorial fights to mock sea battles for which the arena was flooded with water. No one knows how this was done. Water may have been brought in huge wooden containers from the aqueduct. The arena was filled with 4 million gallons (15 million liters) of water; sluice gates were opened to drain it. Emperor Domitian added a basement level, the hypogeum. These tunnels held wild animals in 32 cages with waiting gladiators. They were winched up into the arena by mechanical elevators.

TECHNICAL SPECS

» It would have taken seven hours to fill the Colosseum with water to a depth of 5 feet (1.5 m).

» The shape of the Colosseum was an ellipse (oval), not a circle, in order to give as many people as possible a good view of the arena.

» During the Roman summer, shade was provided by a series of awnings at the top of the structure, supported by 240 wooden masts and a system of ropes and stays.

» Seating reflected social position. The senators and rich people sat in the front rows.

» Arched vaults on the ground floor provided separate entrances numbered from 1 to 80.

HADRIAN'S WALL

The Romans built a wall across northern Britain between C.E. 122 and 128. It was a marvel of technology. Emperor Hadrian had it built to defend the border of the Roman province of Britain from attack by peoples in what is now Scotland. It stretched from coast to coast: a distance of 80 Roman miles (73 miles/118 km).

The wall followed natural features, such as these crags. In the foreground are the ruins of a milecastle.

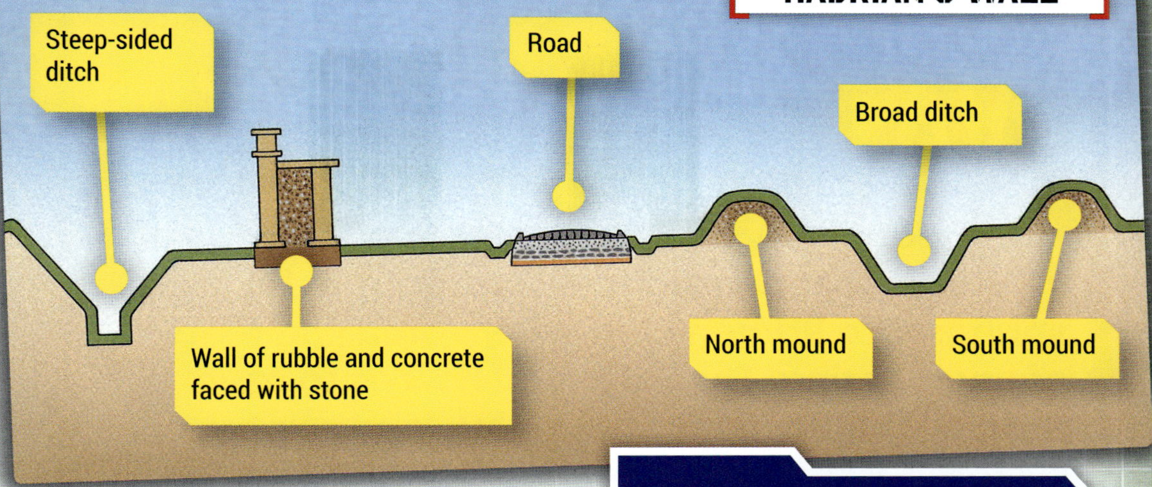

Large sections of the wall survive intact, proving the quality of the original building. The wall was built by soldiers from three Roman legions who used natural features, such as crags, to make it virtually impregnable. It took six years to build in the harsh climate of northern Britain; larger forts were added later.

DEFENDING THE BORDER

Gates were set into the wall at regular intervals. They allowed northern peoples to pass through in order to trade, if they were unarmed. There were turrets every 540 yards (495 m), milecastles every Roman mile, and large forts at intervals of about 7 miles (11 km). About 11,500 soldiers manned the wall until the fall of the Roman Empire in the fifth century.

TECHNICAL SPECS

- **The original plan was for a wall 10 feet (3.3 m) wide and 12 feet (4 m) tall; much of the finished wall was lower and narrower, although in places it reached a height of nearly 20 feet (6 m).**
- **The wall was built of rubble and concrete finished with limestone.**
- **The width of the wall varies along its length.**
- **The walls had ditches on either side. The vallum—the broader ditch—lay behind the wall.**
- **Because the wall followed the landscape's natural contours, it was rarely straight.**
- **A series of 80 milecastles stand at intervals of approximately 1 Roman mile along its length.**

WATERCOURSES

Aqueducts, systems of watercourses and pipes that carried fresh water from lakes or springs into Roman cities, were amazing feats of engineering. They allowed homes to have running water, indoor plumbing, and sewerage systems. Water was stored in the cities in huge tanks and then fed into houses through a series of lead pipes.

The Pont du Gard was built in Gaul—now southern France—by Emperor Trajan in the first century C.E.

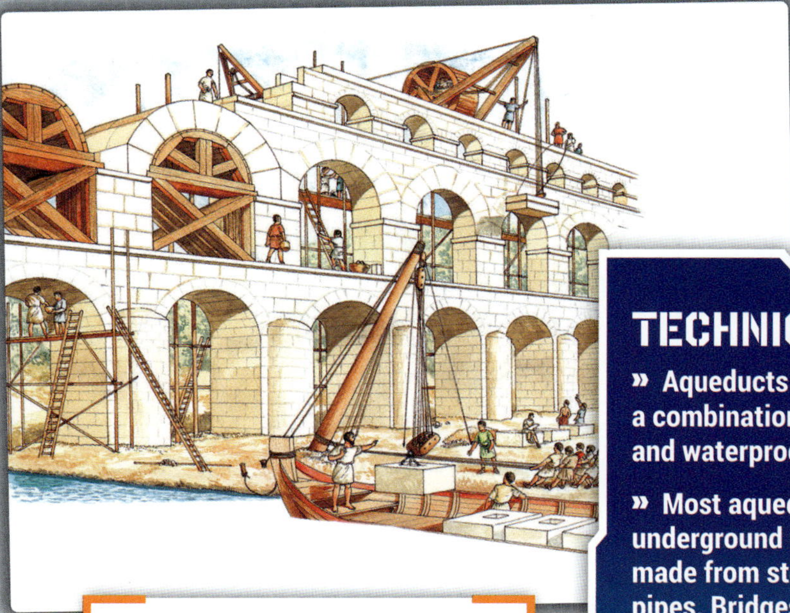

Aqueducts aboveground were built in layers. The top level carried water; a lower level sometimes carried a road.

TECHNICAL SPECS

- Aqueducts were built from a combination of stone, brick, and waterproof cement.
- Most aqueducts were underground water channels made from stone and terracotta pipes. Bridges were built overground if there were obstacles in the way. Most aqueducts were less than 3 feet (1 m) belowground. They were easy to maintain.
- The Aqua Claudia carried water from two springs over 43.75 miles (70 km) into Rome.
- The Pont du Gard in France had a gentle slope; it dropped only 56 feet (17 m) vertically along its length of 30 miles (50 km).

The Romans borrowed the idea of aqueducts from the Etruscans and Greeks. But the Roman system marked a leap forward in water management. Some 500 miles (800 km) of aqueducts fed the city of Rome.

GRAVITY AND BRIDGES

Aqueducts worked by using a gentle downward gradient and gravity to carry water from springs and lakes. Most were underground conduits, which kept the water cool and clean. Where it was too difficult to dig into the ground, aqueducts were built aboveground. When the path crossed a valley, the Romans built high multi-arched bridges, with the water channel at the top.

PUBLIC BATHS

The Roman baths at Bath in England were built on a hot spring. The buildings were updated in the early 19th century by the Georgians.

Unless they were very wealthy, few Romans had private baths in their homes. Instead, they visited the public baths or thermae. These were public spaces where people went to meet and relax, as well as to get clean; the baths were usually set out around a garden, and were carefully engineered.

Once they were undressed, bathers entered a very hot bathroom (caldarium). Soap was expensive, so most bathers covered themselves in olive oil. They scraped the oil and dirt off their skin using curved metal tools called strigils. They then passed through a warm room (tepidarium) before plunging into cold water (frigidarium).

HEAT AND STEAM

Fresh water was fed into the baths through pipes from the nearest cistern. For the warm and hot baths, water was heated in boilers. Some baths also used hypocausts to create steam rooms.

TECHNICAL SPECS

» Some baths used water from natural hot springs, which was diverted by pipes into the buildings; they included the famous baths at Aqua Sulis in Bath, England.

» Slaves kept furnaces burning to keep the air hot or warm.

» Where there were no hot springs, boilers were used to store water; the caldarium boiler was closest to the fire, the tepidarium boiler further away, and the frigidarium boiler furthest away.

» Hot air circulated beneath the floor and in the walls of the caldarium; the floor was so hot bathers had to wear wooden clogs.

BATHS OF POMPEII

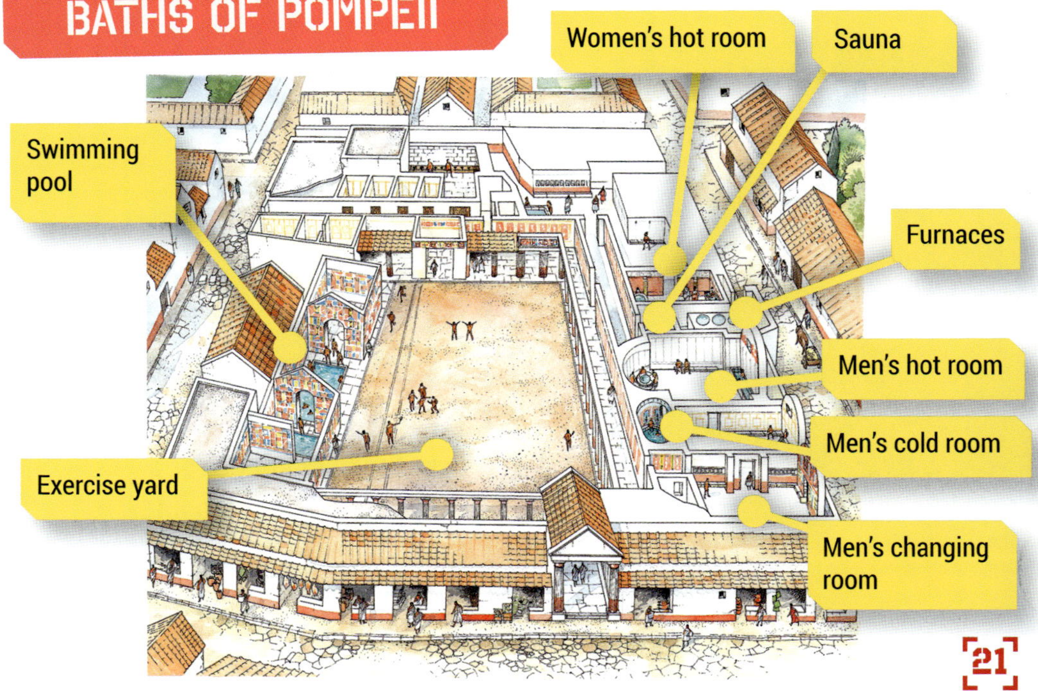

FLOUR MILLS

Bread was an essential food for Romans. It was eaten daily throughout the empire. Traditionally, ancient peoples used animal power to grind grain into flour. When the growing population needed more food, the Romans began using waterpower to turn the millstones.

The Romans worked out the best shape for a millstone. They also knew how quickly it should rotate to be most efficient.

LARGEST MILL IN THE EMPIRE

The mill at Barbegal, near Arles in southern France, was the largest mill complex in the empire. It was built during the second century C.E. and comprised 16 watermills in eight pairs, running down the side of a hill from an aqueduct. The water ran from mill to mill and into a drain at the bottom of the hill. Enough flour could be milled to feed the whole population of Arles, which at the time was about 12,500 people.

MILLS AT BARBEGAL

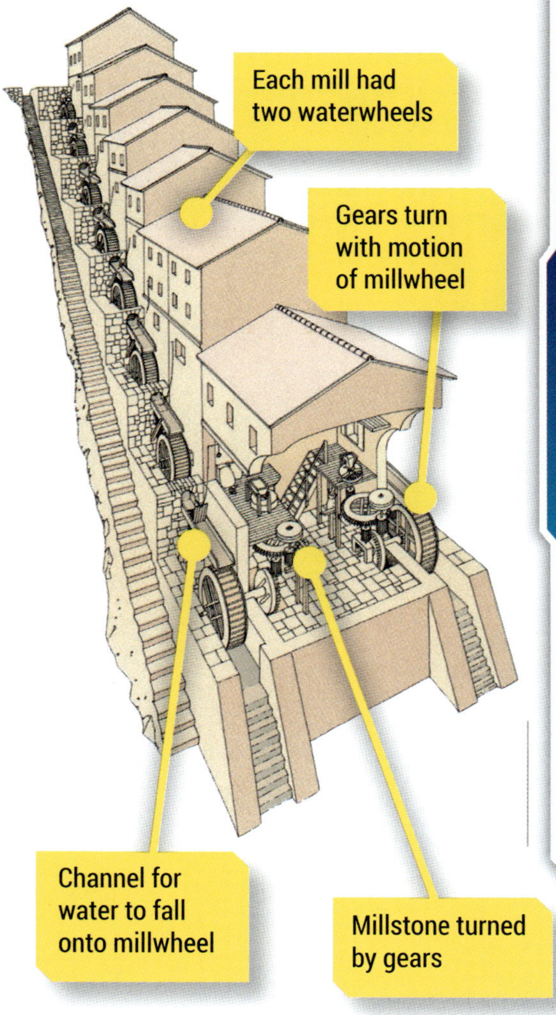

TECHNICAL SPECS

» The Romans adopted watermills from the Greeks, but improved upon the technology.

» Watermills were turned either by water flowing from above (overshot mills) or flowing in a stream beneath the wheel (undershot mills).

» The energy of the wheels was transmitted by a gear mechanism to millstones.

» The Romans changed the shape of millstones, which became wider and squatter; the faces of the stones that rubbed together became smaller.

» Roman millstones were made of basalt; the rock has natural grooves and edges that helped grind the grain more finely.

CONNECTIONS

At its height, the Roman Empire was vast. Reliable communications were essential to government and trade. Goods were transported on the famous Roman network of roads or by boat. On foot people could walk between 12 and 15 miles (20–25 km) a day on the well-made roads; a horse-drawn cart could cover up to 35 miles (50 km) a day.

Horses were vital to communcations. They pulled carts and also provided a postal service that traveled 145 miles (230 km) a day.

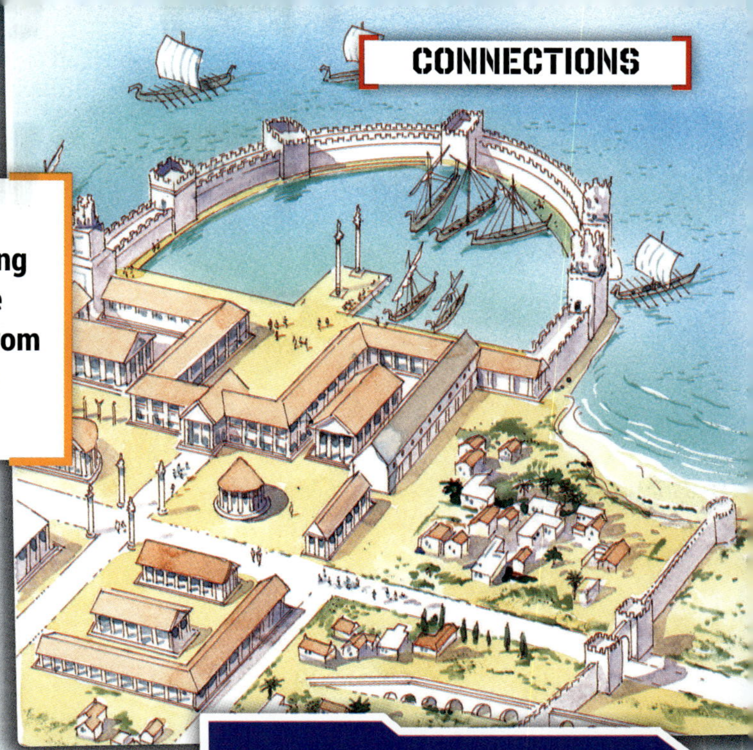

The Romans built harbors for unloading ships such as those that carried grain from North Africa across the Mediterranean.

For short journeys, slaves carried goods on their backs. Carts pulled by oxen were used in the countryside. Soldiers, politicians, traders, and tourists all traveled widely. If they did not know where they were going, they used an itinerarium. These early maps listed places and the distances between them.

SUMMER SAILINGS

During the summer months large ships crossed the seas laden with goods. Sailing could be dangerous, however. There were no compasses and shipwrecks were common because ships sailed close to the coast whenever possible. Pirate raids were no longer a threat, however, as the Romans had brought peace across the Mediterranean.

TECHNICAL SPECS

» The Romans built canals to move freight; the canal that connected Portus, at the mouth of the River Tiber, with Rome's port at Ostia was 100 yards (90 m) wide.

» Chariots and carts had wheels made from iron.

» Horse-drawn coaches (*raeda*) could carry up to 1,000 Roman libra (720 pounds/327 kg) of people and luggage; they were box-shaped and were covered with a cloth roof to shelter the passengers.

ROAD NETWORK

Roman roads followed straight lines set out by surveyors using a sighting stick called a *groma*.

As the Roman Empire expanded from the fourth century B.C.E., the Romans built a network of roads to connect their sprawling empire. They were used for trade and official communications, but also for the speedy movement of armies in times of trouble. They were well built, and many remain beneath modern roads to this day.

ROADS TO ROME

The heart of the road network was Rome itself. Roads radiated out from the city toward all points of the empire. The first, the Appian Way, was built in 312 B.C.E. It ran south from Rome. Other important road hubs were Lyon in Gaul (France) and London in Britain. By the height of the empire in the first century C.E., Roman roads stretched across Europe, North Africa, and the Middle East, from the Atlantic Ocean in the west to the Euphrates River in the east. The road system comprised 50,000 miles (80,000 km) of highways.

TECHNICAL SPECS

» Roads were often built by work gangs of soldiers.

» The engineers first dug parallel drainage ditches about 40 feet (12 m) apart.

» They cleared a trench between them as a roadbed.

» They laid a foundation of stone slabs, covered with sand or mortar. They added a layer of crushed stones.

» On top they laid stone slabs or cobbles in mortar, which allowed rainwater to drain through into the drainage ditches.

» Large roads were often lined by curb stones up to 8 inches (20 cm) high on either side.

HOW TO...

The layered structure of Roman roads gave them great stability, which is one reason why some still survive more than 2,000 years after they were built. The surface stones allowed rainwater to drain into ditches at either side of the roadway.

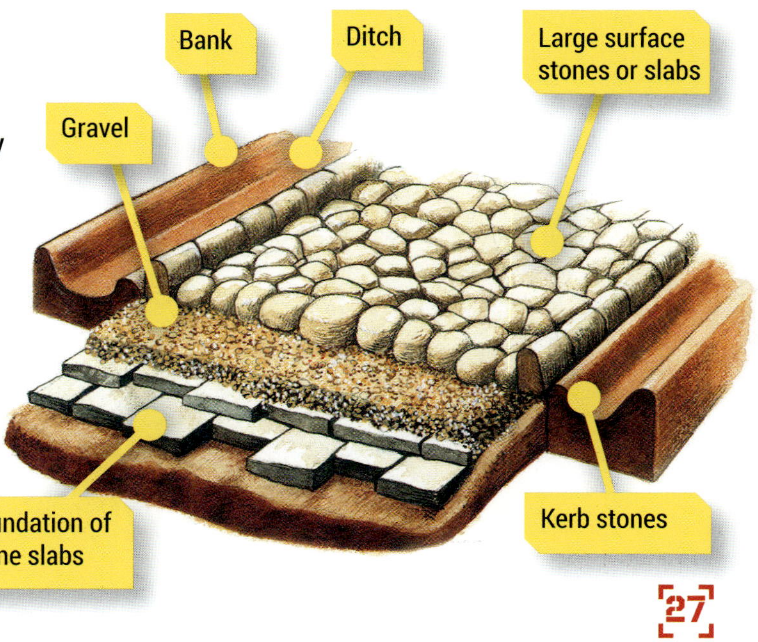

SHIPBUILDING

The ancient Romans adopted shipbuilding techniques first used in ancient Greece. Roman merchant ships carried cargo throughout a network of trade routes across the empire, and Rome's dominance of the Mediterranean was enforced by warships propelled by hundreds of rowers.

MERCHANT SHIP

Rome's empire relied on merchant ships, or *corbitas*. They transported wheat, wine, oil, and cloth. The ships carried large wooden goose heads that represented the Egyptian goddess Isis, the guardian of seafarers.

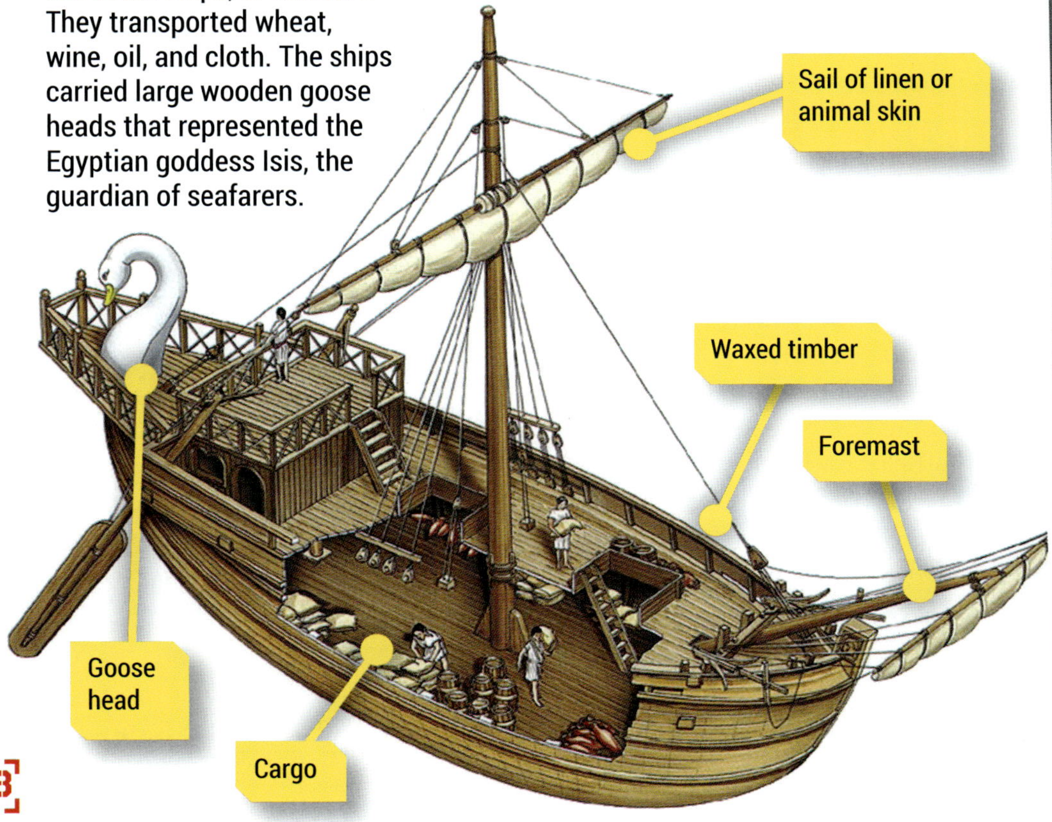

Some galleys had a drawbridge on deck. It was used to board enemy ships, but the added weight made the ship unstable.

The main cargo vessel was the corbita. It had a rounded hull and a curved prow and stern. The corbita was a slow, clumsy vessel, but it was very seaworthy. It could sail as far as India and carry loads of up to 385 tons (350 tonnes).

WARSHIPS

The standard Roman warship was the quinquereme. This had five rowers to each oar, and a total crew of about 300 men. The quinquereme galleys were rowed at high speed into enemy ships. A ram at the ship's prow holed the enemy ship underwater, while marines rushed across ramps.

TECHNICAL SPECS

» Shipbuilders laid the keel first, then added the planks of the hull.

» The planks were joined closely edge to edge with mortise-and-tenon joints.

» The hulls were made waterproof with wax, tarred fabric, or lead sheets.

» The largest cargo ships were grain carriers that brought corn from Egypt. When used for passengers, grain ships could carry up to 600 people.

» The average speed of a merchant ship was 3.5 knots (4 mph/6.5 kmh). A galley could be rowed at speeds of up to 12 knots (14 mph/22 kmh).

FARMS

A slave shepherd watches his sheep while other slaves harvest olives (right), pick grapes (left), and plow the land (center).

The Roman economy was based on agriculture. The main crops were wheat, grapes, and olives. Bread was a vital food across the empire, and grain was also traded with the wider world. At the height of the empire, many small farms had been absorbed into large estates (latifundia) that were worked by slaves who provided a cheap source of labor.

Land was prepared for crops by using oxen to pull plows. Early *ard* plows were little more than sharp sticks. The Romans added an extra blade named a coulter, which broke up the ground in front of the plow's cutting blade. Crops were originally harvested by hand, using sickles, but in the first century C.E., a reaping machine named the *vallus* was invented.

CROP ROTATION

The Romans practiced crop rotation and mixed farming. This allowed the soil to rest, so that it did not become too depleted of nutrients by overuse of the land.

TECHNICAL SPECS

» The Romans grew emmer, an ancient type of wheat that had twice as much protein as modern wheat.

» Wheat cultivation was labor intensive; wheat had to be cut, threshed and winnowed to separate the grain, and the grain had to be stored. The Romans introduced machines for various stages of the task.

» Vast amounts of forest were cleared across the Roman Empire to make way for farmland.

» Grapes were pressed to make wine either by foot or by using a mechanical screw press.

» The Romans introduced olive cultivation across their empire.

MACHINERY

MECHANICAL REAPER (Vallus)

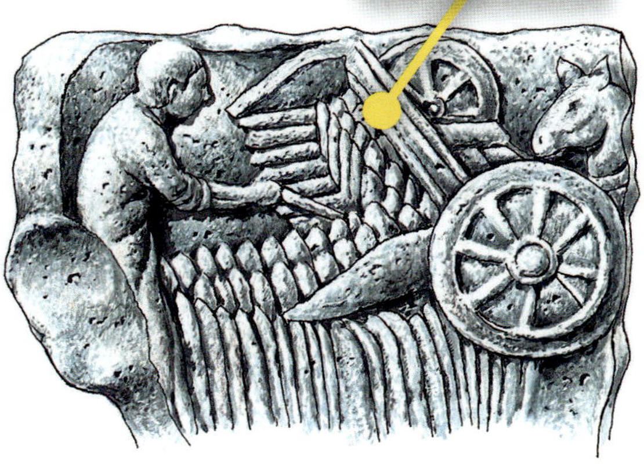

PLOWS

The ard (above) had a metal tip to turn the soil. Romans in Gaul developed another type of plow (above right). This had a coulter in front of the plowshare that could dig and turn the heavier soils of northern Europe.

MILITARY EQUIPMENT

The Roman army was the most efficient military force in the ancient world. It was the backbone of the Roman Empire, using its strength to conquer and control other tribes, clans, and empires. Roman soldiers used axes, spears, daggers, and swords. Larger weapons were used to besiege enemy cities, an important part of Roman wafare.

BODY ARMOR

Roman soldiers wore flexible armor made from overlapping iron scales that were hinged at the back and fastened together at the front. The armor plates were held together by straps of leather. Helmets were based on Celtic designs and were made from bronze. Soldiers carried an oval shield made of wood and covered with linen and calfskin. Iron strips on the shield protected against sword thrusts.

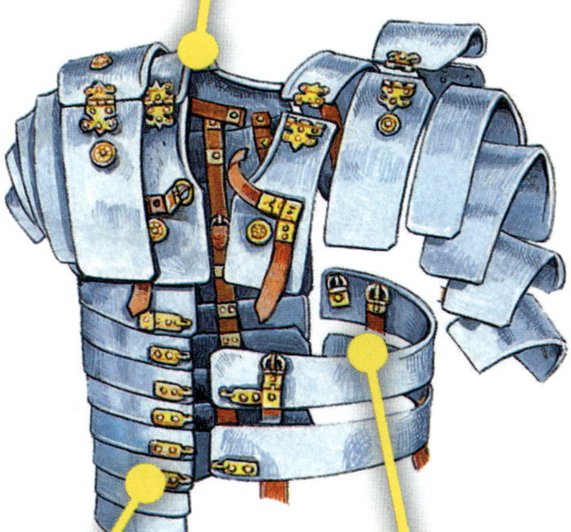

The Romans built siege engines that they wheeled up to city walls. There were iron-tipped battering rams (aries) and boring drills (terebras). There were also tall wooden towers from which soldiers could climb onto the walls via a drawbridge. Among other large-scale weapons were the ballista, a massive crossbow that fired flaming arrows or pointed bolts, and the onager, a catapult that threw stone balls up to 1,400 feet (425 m).

PERSONAL WEAPONS

For close fighting, a Roman soldier was equipped with a metal-covered shield (scutum), a sword (gladius), a metal-tipped spear (pilium), a bronze helmet, and metal armor.

BALLISTA

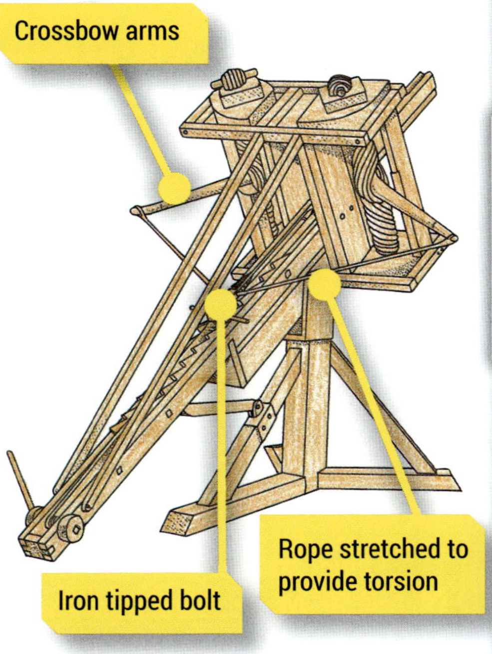

TECHNICAL SPECS

- Roman weapons were often based on Greek originals.
- Onagers were sometimes used to throw clay balls filled with a combustible substance; when the clay broke, the ball burst into flames.
- The scutum was curved to protect the soldier's sides as well as his front; it was 40 inches (1 m) tall and 30 inches (75 cm) wide.
- Soldiers used their shields to form a "tortoise," a formation in which shields were held over the head to form a protective shell.
- Artillery and towers were used to lay siege to enemy cities.

MEASURES AND WEIGHTS

The Roman Empire was based on trade between different peoples over long distances. It was therefore important to standardize a system of weights and measures that could be used for trade and construction throughout Roman territory. The most important unit was probably the Roman mile.

The Romans were the first peoples to use the word mile (Latin mille, or "a thousand"). It referred to a thousand paces. The mile was used to mark distances on Roman roads and to decide where to position fortifications. No one knows exactly how long a Roman mile was, but it was probably nearly 5,000 feet (1,520 m).

This vessel was used to measure a unit of volume called a modius; weights and measures were controlled by the empire.

The groma had weights on its four arms to help the surveyor make sure it was vertical.

TECHNICAL SPECS

» The base unit for weight was the uncia, which was equivalent to 1 ounce (28 g); 12 uncia equaled 1 libra (12 ounces/336 g).

» The base unit of dry and liquid volume was the sextarius; 1 sextarius measured between 0.56–0.61 quart (0.53–0.58 l).

» The Roman mile was based on 1,000 paces—but the precise length of a pace is unknown.

» A Roman foot measured 11.6 inches (29.6 cm).

» Road distances were marked from the "golden milepost" (Milliarium Aureum) in the Forum in Rome.

» Surveyors used carts equipped with toothed gearwheels to measure distances along roads; every mile, the gearwheel pushed a pebble into a container.

SURVEYING

One of the uses of Roman measurements was surveying. Surveyors marked out roads, fortifications, and the sites of bridges and cities. They used measuring sticks and simple tools. The groma—two crossed sticks on top of a vertical staff—helped to work out straight lines and right angles. Calculation was used to work out, for example, the gradient of an aqueduct.

CHANGING TIME AND SPACE

The old lunar calendar was based on the cycles of the moon. It had 12 months, and the year was 355 days long. But this lunar year was out of step with the solar year. Romans made the change from a calendar based on the moon to one based on the sun.

In late Roman times Ptolemy came up with an inaccurate but influential view of the universe.

The sundial arrived from Sicily in 236 B.C.E. The Romans used it to divide the daylight into 12 roughly equal periods—hours.

By the first century B.C.E., the calendar was out by a season. Astronomers had known for two centuries that a true year was 365.2 days long. In 46 B.C.E, Julius Caesar, introduced a solar calendar. It had 365 days a year and an extra day every four years.

FAMOUS ASTRONOMER

Ptolemy was a Greek–Roman who worked in Alexandria, Egypt, between C.E. 127 and 145. He described a planetary system with the Earth at its center. His work influenced astronomers for the next 1,400 years. It was the basis for all Roman astronomy.

TECHNICAL SPECS

- Late in the Roman Empire, the Romans divided history at the birth of Christ: Before Christ (B.C.) and Anno Domini (A.D.), which means "in the year of our lord."
- Before the solar calendar could be introduced, the discrepancies that had built up from the lunar calendar needed to be ironed out, so the previous year had 445 days.
- The new calendar is known as the Julian Calendar, for the emperor Julius Caesar.
- Many of our names for months come from the Roman calendar.
- Like the Egyptians and Greeks, the Romans used sundials to tell the time of day.

CLOTH AND DYES

Everyone needed cloth for clothing, from the beautiful imported silk and cotton favored by the rich to the hemp wool clothing worn by peasants. Workers spun yarn, wove textiles, and used dyes to color the fabric. As with the cloth itself, colors varied according to wealth.

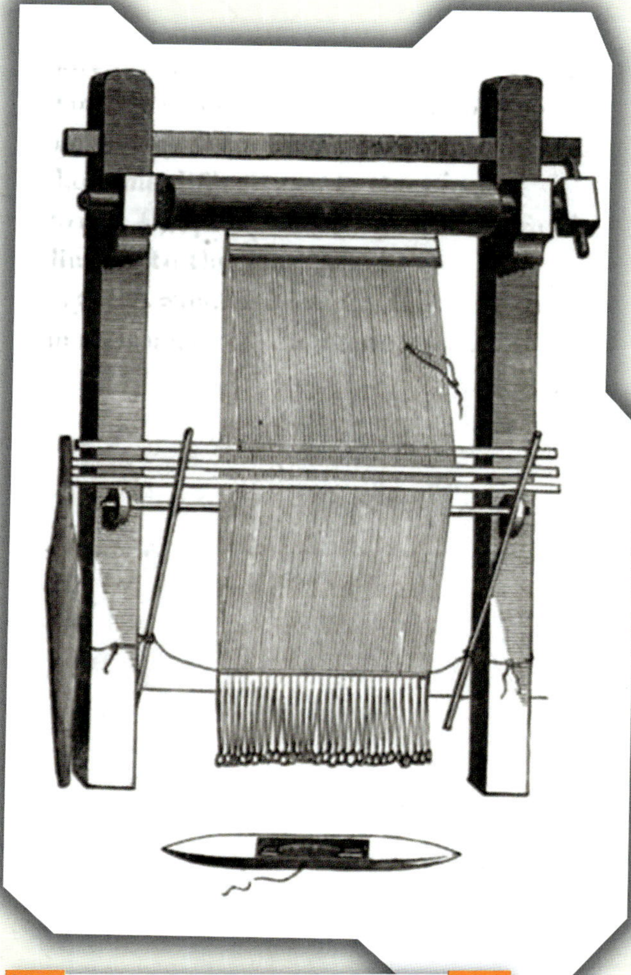

The Romans used upright warp-weighted looms. Lead weights tied to the end of the hanging threads kept the threads tight.

The most common material was wool, but linen and hemp were also widely used. Silk was imported from China and fine cotton came from India. Preparing wool was time consuming. The fleece was washed in water and then dried. Once the fibers were dried, they had to be pressed and smoothed before they could be woven.

TYRIAN PURPLE

Dyes came from different sources and varied widely in cost. Tyrian purple was named for Tyre in Lebanon, where it was produced from a mollusk. It was so expensive to produce that it was originally worn only by the emperor.

TECHNICAL SPECS

» Cloth was woven on vertical looms at home; poor women wove for their own families, while the wealthy used slaves to do the weaving.

» To keep clothes white, they were often washed in a solution that included urine.

» The most highly prized wool came from the sheep of Tarentum in southern Italy.

» Most dyes were from plants, and there was a relatively limited selection. Saffron produced yellow, while the madder plant produced various shades of red.

» The most common source of blue dye was indigo, obtained from plants in Asia.

» Iron alum was used as a fixing agent for dyes.

Mollusks from Lebanon produced Tyrian purple; the dye was so valuable some people bought fake versions.

USING METAL

The Romans used metal to make tools, coins, and statues. Although there were mines in Italy, the area around Rome had few sources of metal, so metals were imported from all over the empire. Gold and silver came from Spain and Greece, tin from Britain, and copper from Spain and Cyprus.

This statue of Marcus Aurelius balances on three of the horse's legs, which was a challenge for the sculptors.

Metals were so scarce that metal objects were often melted down and reused. The Romans adopted coins from Greece. Roman coinage was introduced in the third century B.C.E. Silver coins minted in Rome were used across the empire.

BRONZE STATUES

One of the most popular subjects for bronze statues was the emperor on a horse. It took great skill to cast an equestrian statue, because all the weight was supported by the horse's slender ankles. Statues of emperors were often melted down after an emperor had died and the bronze was reused for the next one.

TECHNICAL SPECS

- Mining was dangerous, so it was done by slaves; they used stone or metal picks to dig out the minerals.
- The Romans used waterwheels to remove water from flooded mines.
- A cheaper substitute for gold was obtained by mixing copper and zinc.
- The Romans reheated iron with carbon to make a stronger metal known as steel.
- Roman coins included the as (bronze), sestertius (a small silver coin), and denarius (a large silver coin). The aureus was a gold coin.
- Only one Roman equestrian statue survives. It shows Emperor Marcus Aurelius on his horse.

This silver coin shows the two-headed god Janus; such designs were added to coins to show they were genuine.

MAKING GLASS

The Romans adopted glass production from the Greeks, who produced highly colored, thick cast glass vessels. However, in the first century C.E. a new technique enabled glass to be blown, resulting in thinner walls. Suddenly glass was being used everywhere: for vases, as tiny squares in mosaics, and even in windows.

The dramatic expansion in the production of Roman glass was due to the introduction of a new technique from Syria. Glassblowing involved heating a ball of glass until it was very soft, then blowing air through a long tube to inflate it into a hollow vessel. Glassblowing had many advantages over previous techniques. It was quicker to blow glass than to cast it,

This blown-glass urn was made before C.E. 300. It held the ashes of someone who had been cremated.

and blown vessels had thinner walls, which meant they used less glass. That in turn meant that more glass was available. Glassware went from being a high-status object to being far more common. The Romans were also recyclers: they melted down broken glass to make new vessels.

PEAK PRODUCTION

Roman glass production reached its peak in the second century C.E. Different styles were produced in different parts of the Roman Empire. Glass became popular for use at the tables of rich Romans. It was easier to clean than pottery vessels, and did not taint the food as bronze vessels did.

TECHNICAL SPECS

» To make glass, the Romans used a furnace to heat a mixture of silica and soda with a stabilizer (usually lime or magnesia).

» Adding specific metal oxides changed the color of the glass.

» Cobalt was added to make dark blue glass.

» Tin was used to produce opaque white glass.

» Manganese oxide was used to make colorless glass.

» From the first century C.E., glass mosaic tiles (tesserae) were manufactured; these were usually yellow, blue, or green.

» Roman glass had a highly shiny surface; examples that still survive today have, not surprisingly, become dull over the centuries.

This glass vessel is shaped like a head. It was made in the second century C.E. in what is now the Balkans.

TIMELINE

B.C.E.

509 The Romans drive the Etruscans out of Rome; they found a republic and begin to conquer Etruscan cities.

347 Coins are introduced into Rome.

312 Roman politician Appius Claudius Caecus builds the Aqua Appia aqueduct.

300 Rome becomes the dominant power in Italy.

250 Roman farmers start using crop rotation.

241 Rome defeats Carthage in the First Punic War and takes control of Sicily.

218 Rome fights Carthage in the Second Punic War (c. 218–201).

204 Rome goes to war against Macedonia; after victory in 205, Rome dominates the western Mediterranean.

170 The world's first paved streets appear in Rome.

146 Rome establishes the province of Africa, taking control of the whole Mediterranean.

110 Romans begin using nailed horseshoes.

100 Roman builders used concrete made from crushed stones and pozzolana (volcanic ash) cement, which sets underwater.

80 Vertical undershot waterwheels are introduced in Mediterranean countries for grinding corn.

58 Julius Caesar begins a 10-year campaign to conquer Gaul (France).

46 Julius Caesar is named dictator for life in Rome. He introduces the Julian calendar.

44 Julius Caesar is assassinated in Rome.

27 Octavian becomes emperor, marking the start of the Roman Empire.

C.E.

20	Pont du Gard built in France.
30	The first Latin treatise on medicine is published.
50	Aqueduct built in Segovia, Spain. Italian farmers use watermills to grind grain.
60	Roman forces in Britain defeat Boudicca, queen of the Iceni tribe.
77	Pliny the Elder summarizes Roman natural history.
79	The volcano Vesuvius erupts, burying the Roman towns of Pompeii and Herculaneum.
80	The Colosseum amphitheater is built in Rome.
117	The Empire reaches its greatest extent under Hadrian.
128	The Pantheon is built in Rome,
150	Roman–Greek geographer Ptolemy compiles a compendium of astronomy.
286	Diocletian divides the empire into western and eastern halves.
300	The palace built for Diocletian in Split uses arches supported by free-standing columns. A mill is built near Arles in France with 16 overshot waterwheels.
312	Roman general Constantine becomes emperor after defeating imperial forces at the battle of Milvian Bridge.
330	Constantine takes the ancient city of Byzantium as his new capital, Constantinople.
350	Romans in France use a water-powered sawmill to cut marble.
410	Barbarian Visigoths, led by Alaric, sack Rome, marking the symbolic fall of the Roman Empire.
441	Attila leads the Huns in a large-scale invasion of the Roman Empire.
476	The German chieftain Odoacer deposes the last western emperor, Romulus Augustulus, marking the end of the empire in the west.

GLOSSARY

amphitheater An oval or circular building with seating for an audience.

aqueduct A channel for carrying water.

ard A simple plow with a sharp point that turns the soil.

basilica A large oblong hall or building with colonnades and domed roof used in ancient Rome for public assemblies.

canal An artificial waterway.

cast To pour molten metal into a mold and allow it to harden.

cistern An underground tank for storing water.

concrete A strong building material made by mixing a powder such as cement with stone and water.

empire A large territory ruled by an emperor or empress.

gladiatorial Related to gladiators, who fought each other for public entertainment.

gradient The angle at which a slope descends.

hemp A plant whose fibers are used to make material.

kiln An oven used to harden pottery or bake bricks.

millstone A large circular stone that rubs against another stone to grind corn into flour.

mosaic A decoration made by using small pieces of colored glass to cover a surface.

rotunda A round building, usually covered with a dome.

sewerage A system of pipes to take away wastewater or sewage.

siege engine A large machine used to attack the walls of a besieged city.

staple A food that makes up the major part of a diet.

strigil A curved metal rod used to scrape the skin.

surveyor Someone who carefully measures the land.

vault An arched structure that forms a ceiling or roof.

FURTHER RESOURCES

BOOKS

Hayes, Lucy D. *How Did Romans Count to 100?* Flowerpot Press, 2022.

Howell, Izzi. *The Genius of the Romans* (Genius of the Ancients). Crabtree Publishing, 2019.

Levy, Janey. *The Feats of Ancient Rome* (That's Ancient!) Gareth Stevens Pub, 2021.

Platt, Richard. *How They Made Things Work: Romans.* Twenty-Franklin Watts, 2021.

Spilsbury, Louise. *Forensic Investigations of the Romans* (Forensic Footprints of Ancient Worlds). Crabtree Publishing, 2018.

Uhl, Wina M. *How STEM Built the Roman Empire* (How STEM Built Empires). Rosen Young Adult, 2019.

WEBSITES

education.nationalgeographic.org/resource/ancient-rome-101
National Geographic video about the story of Ancient Rome and its technological achievements.

www.history.com/news/10-innovations-that-built-ancient-rome
Information on 10 innovations that shaped ancient Rome.

www.bbc.co.uk/history/ancient/romans/tech_01.shtml
BBC site that asks "What did the Romans ever do for us?"

historyforkids.org/ancient-rome-the-romans-facts-information-for-kids/
History for Kids page with links about Roman architecture.

INDEX